SEEING THE BODY

SEEING THE BODY

Poems

RACHEL ELIZA GRIFFITHS

W. W. NORTON & COMPANY

Independent Publishers Since 1923

For information about permission to reproduce selections from this book, write to
Permissions, W. W. Norton & Company, Inc., 500 Fifth Avenue, New York, NY 10110

For information about special discounts for bulk purchases, please contact
W. W. Norton Special Sales at specialsales@wwnorton.com or 800-233-4830

Manufacturing by Versa Press
Book design by Chris Welch Design
Production manager: Julia Druskin

Library of Congress Cataloging-in-Publication Data

Names: Griffiths, Rachel Eliza, author.
Title: Seeing the body : poems / Rachel Eliza Griffiths.
Description: First edition. | New York : W. W. Norton & Company, [2020]
Identifiers: LCCN 2020007885 | ISBN 9781324005667 (hardcover) |
ISBN 9781324005674 (epub)
Subjects: LCGFT: Poetry.
Classification: LCC PS3607.R5494 S44 2020 | DDC 811/.6—dc23
LC record available at https://lccn.loc.gov/2020007885

W. W. Norton & Company, Inc., 500 Fifth Avenue, New York, N.Y. 10110
www.wwnorton.com

W. W. Norton & Company Ltd., 15 Carlisle Street, London W1D 3BS

1 2 3 4 5 6 7 8 9 0

In Love & Praise of My Mother

Michele Antoinette Pray-Griffiths

August 31, 1954–July 28, 2014

Did you know you're loved by somebody?

—STEVIE WONDER, "AS"

contents

daughter: lyric: landscape

good death

author's note

The self-portraits in the section of this book entitled "daughter: lyric: landscape" function as a map of the self and of the greater world in which I am both visualized and invisible, as a symptom of grief and identity. This series of photographs includes self-portraits created just days before and immediately after my mother's death, as well as other self-portraits created on the first-year anniversary of her passing. Self-portraits were created in the space of my first artists' residency following her death as well as the residency during which this writing was completed. Specific places where these images were created include Oxford and Gloster, Mississippi; Santa Fe, New Mexico; Captiva, Florida; and Saratoga Springs, New York. It is my choice to provide neither title nor date for any of the images, though of course I could and call it factual. But the provision of a specific kind of literal architecture would undercut the truth of these images, which is that they are of myself—woman as ghost, woman as body, geography, and imagination, woman as a self, as a resistance, that is ever tense in the progression of frames, woman in the perpetuity of language, and woman in the sanctity of intuition. I am looking at a woman whose spirit is both emaciated and exhilarated in the face of monumental loss.

mother: mirror: god

SEEING THE BODY

She died & I—
In the spring of her blood, I remember
my mother's first injury. Surprise of unborn
petals curling red, then dark around her wrist.
Some fruit she cut, some onion, some
body with skin & sharp seeds. She fed me.
She lived Us & I—
She held We & I—
She kept speaking with those flowers
falling from her blood, taking her
across the sky to death. I remember
her voice like a horn I never want
to pull out of my heart. In the next life,
which is here & here, I gather every mouth
that ever sang my mother's blues.
She burned & I—
She talked back hard at god.
O, my mother, she danced unbroken too.
Bale of grief on my back, opening
into something black I wear. A life of flesh
like a petal or fruit or burning.
I've carried everything & I'm tired.
My mother survived & I—
        (But she did not live).
She told me Nothing & I—
She was waiting the entire time.
How does the elegy believe me?
Together, we crossed the sky.
There was a gate & we walked through
the world like that.

She wrote We & I—
She was last or never seen, & I—
Brown eyes, without life, opened her
eternity. When the air in her stopped
                           & I—
She was last seen dying. She was too silent
for the first time in her life. The spring of
my mother's blood hot & god the dark
dark beyond the closed door
that won't move again.

VOLUME

On guard my mother studied her
ankles & hands all the time. Any swelling
set off alarms. Everything in our home
bolted to wet silence. Our family
could be capsized should the fluid
breach her heart. More than once
it did. Surrounded her heart
with gold liquid. Attacked her
heart with its rising flood.
I hated the smell & arrogance
of it. The way pain misshaped
my mother's lovely muscles.
I never understood how
the body made so much of it.
She would pull fluid off her body.
Concerned for the kidney
she had received from a murdered child.
Worried that the fluid would pull her
under the hull of her own organs.
Liters & milliliters placed us
on the brink. For years after she died
I lived along a gold, raw edge
of Maybe or Maybe Not. I kept asking:
Could I have ever saved her?
I only mean that some days I was certain
there was nothing left after she died
that could fill the hollows in me. I wanted to
know how I could drown my Ishmael
of memory. Lift my life out of my mother's
mute grave. Nothing to surround my heart,

which turned & kicked like something
orphaned in its cradle. Red-veined rage
burning itself blue with screaming.
I was so sick last January my doctors
ordered iron, multiple blood transfusions.
My blood was bad, giving up its blue air.
Yet I refused new blood. Having sacrificed
my blood to my mother's absence,
I could barely stand to give myself
the anchor of blood that might pull me
above the waves, those lost years I drifted
like an empty bottle under the tide.

HOUSE

Pavarotti trembled across the terse
sunlight of every room. Opera music plashed
shining hardwood floors. A plastic bucket of
hot water & bleach steaming in peace, the ugly rag
clenched in my mother's fist like a rose.
She would never stop cleaning our corners, our walls,
the windows, the doorknobs. On her knees searching
for the one speck of filth another woman might notice.
Lemon Pledge baptized polished banisters.
Roasted chicken or homemade spaghetti
with garlic bread. Sloppy Joes. Who remembers that
delicious mess? Those years we children grew devoutly
in our mother's love. A feast of discipline & delight.
Inside silent moments, she smiled like a shy girl
& urged us to turn up The Supremes or Smokey Robinson.
She used to go to Howard Theatre in Washington,
where she was born, and see Stevie Wonder, Otis Redding.
We always wanted to please her. We lip-synced, fumbling
The Miracles & The Temptations. Spinning in a home
of sugar & sweetness, we danced whenever we could.
I remembered Smokey & Luciano Pavarotti
going back & forth through the proud, warbled
chambers of my childhood. My mother pushed me
into an asylum of books. Hid her own daring
escape inside stacks of etiquette manuals.
A young black mother scrubbing love songs
across the drama of ordinary life.
Her eyes sparkled from soap, longing, lack,
& tears she never shared. She fed us her ghost

stories while fading inside her body, her beliefs.
We chewed hope, fear, rage. Her soul
music cleaned us raw & good. All those days
scraped with a sad future that was gaining
on us like a voice.

CHRONOLOGY

I don't remember when her name begins
          in the world. I forget what maiden word

the water

          made against my mother's tongue. Unbroken thirst. Black
          earth. Darkness, singing blue & green. Fruit trees of her hands.

Animals roar her blood into bright air. Ghosts scrape brown rivers
upon her skin. The teeth of the dead tear her unborn words into rafts.

My mother's maiden name is Pray. She is a pure being of
blood, promise, trouble. Perhaps, I was there, gaining details.

Wonder corrodes our armor of ribs & speech. Contours breaching
the wave that will widow our family. Her breath going down &

staying beneath its darkest tongue. The water recalling who
the earth believed she was before the god. I want to open

my mother's dead hands & listen. Let the human record show
our slant of suffering. Let cum & rain lash chokecherry leaves

with desire, pain, imagination. Show me how the art of losing
masters each morning. The mind of

          the earth turned like a heart after death.

Our wounds took the form of night.
Our fears rocked like white, tearful waves against the last ships.

Our mothers rolled like shells under the raging sea.
Which means, by what I must write in blood—

    my naked hand labored through the bruised dark to speak.

Which means language is neither innocent nor
free. A woman swells alone inside mauve fields.

A grief makes its own blood. *The petals beneath me*

                          have already changed.

The wound of life gave the night endless
       shame & would not close its mouth.

ARCH OF HYSTERIA,
OR, THE SPIDER-MOTHER BECOMES A WOMAN

I have been to hell and back.
And let me tell you, it was wonderful.

—LOUISE BOURGEOIS

I want my web to hold. I want to repair
what I have made. I was not given the gold hive.
In me seethes the silk of invisible worlds. Spinning
my hairline body within emptiness, I project
our unwoven path. I dangle above filaments
of what the body must eat, must make. Each morning
my life reels from unclear lines of mud, plaster. Love is
whatever you think you can carry from your childhood
without breaking your heart. There's a silent prayer
that matters to this girl, to that mother, to all of
my daughters who are at work. The wind blows us
against each day. We birth a word or silence.
We snap threads impatiently with our teeth.
Pleasure sends us in & out of silken traps
we make then abandon. Ensnared by
the fatigue of our masters, shamed by the duel
of Athena & Arachne, we ignore our myths.
We work to feed our victories. Our sex
clings to the map of the web, the sperm set
upon gossamer threads until we are prepared.
We, who do not touch but only open, we,
whose children don't remember what it took
for us to free ourselves. Wingless & certain, we fly.
I am ether by the time you find a trace of
me. The gift of my legs spread intricately
from post to beam to corner. Your cells,

upon closer inspection, resemble my descendants.
Cast me into love or flames but do not leave me
alone in your house. It will only take me
moments to haunt the body you have
orphaned. That clot you call a soul.
I make my way out of the socket
of your eye, where you once held me
in horror & awe. We crawl together
along the tripwire of my hungers
to the center of what I have done
to feed myself, my children.

MYTH

July 25, 2014
Oxford, Mississippi

When a nurse in Philadelphia
says my mother can no longer speak,
six blackbirds in the Oxford cemetery
arrive. Their brittle songs hang from
the silence of wide trees where I am
walking near Faulkner's grave. Pallbearers
with black wings, their shadows cast
a sudden twilight against the white
stones where the dead forever perch
in memory. Here is the appalling
song climbing up from the music
of my eyes. Birds, blackbirds, black
& mute, fly with no meaning

      but return.

The entire month there were storms,
savage enough to fear.

Who told these terrible oaks I was once
a woman, a fear, a song? Who gave me this
blinding beauty but those scavengers?

Ropes of blood swing in the dying
glare of the oak's memory.

I watch a doe & fawn cross
the lawn of the dead. In hunger, the animals
nudge the headstones they know
by smell. In my waking dreams their hunger
is a mouth praying

for the ache of salt upon my palms. Did I cry
like the sea when I was born? Did I mimic
the sound of the beast I was at the beginning
or the animal I would become?

I am daughter of the sun, am moonlit bride of
a lyric that forces me to sing, to bite
the snake again, after it has freed me. A woman
who has looked for justice
in her lover's eye.

Did I ever find it?

Here in Mississippi, I see & heed
every flag, honey, cinder. You know it
means the oaks are singing
into the dreams of grief-broken
prisoners. The moonlight struck
my skin last night for proof

I had been born at all.

Crossing the street I hold my mother's trouble
near my ear. I wait for news. In the meadow
of dying I kneel & spin above the unholy puddles
of love's drowning. It is nearly musical—

the message—
under waves of light falling away
to clear stars. The sea & blood
at twilight have the same cost.

Each god tells death to look
at my face. My mother's nickname
for me was Face. That was all
I heard scuttling its cry

deep across red dunes in my ears. My mother
calling to me through the quickening
of her death. Face, Face.

> *Come, quickly. Eurydice, sing*
> *our grief,* the gods say. *Sing us the music*
> *of justice, strike the snake before you die*
> *so that you will have the knowledge*
> *of the Underworld.*

My shadow offered to love,
to Orpheus. My kisses stolen between the breasts
of the earth & my broken breastbone.

The shadow of the world looking back
where hell held a love song.

Your mother cannot speak,
a nurse says on the phone.
She cannot tell you
anything.

COMEDY

I am here before the nurse brings my mother breakfast.
I study her body. Try to remember if I caught my mother
in the dream I had the night before where the hem of her
gown flew through a silver tunnel without end. Her skin
went right through my hands whenever I was close enough
to save her. She slipped through her name, her name I could not stop
calling until I sat up alone in my crib. Embarrassed, she tells me
she remembers how she phoned me last night to let me know
she was in the morgue. She laughs as the nurse, whose feet squeak
in Minnie Mouse Crocs, arrives with tea. We watch the nurse
with eyes that will never remember her face. Thank her
for the toast that is thicker than my mother's hand.
That morphine is some powerful shit, my mother says.
I agree with her as though she has merely mentioned it is cold
outside though I have rarely had morphine &
have never made courtesy calls from a morgue. *It was late*
& I didn't know where I was, she says. *Because that wasn't death,*
which means I couldn't have called you from that place.
This is my new mother who has finally admitted fear
into the raw ward of her heart. This is my mother who flew away
from my grasp in the tunnel without end. The woman
who could not wait for me to grab the white edge
of where she was going. *I was afraid,* she says. Looking
over the rim of her plastic cup, she shakes the world. Chipped
ice between us. *Yeah don't go & write about me like that,*
she says. *I already know you will.*

BELIEF

I'd come into the room & try to write
a different ending on those anonymous walls.
There was less time all the time
until time changed. You know what I mean.
You stare at the clock, the vomit-hued walls, that
hush dripping in your head until you feel
you have never been elsewhere. Your world
is a sigh from the bed. A moan. Another request
for ice chips. Water. Some news, any news
from the doctor. Water, again. Where is the doctor?
I tried to read & write. Over & over, I
arranged plain little soaps, toothbrush, & comb.
From home I brought her own things: hairbrush,
Dove & Revlon lipstick. Dolled our darling up.
Washed her weary face. Hair twisted into a ballerina bun.
Used the Pink Lotion the way I was taught, rubbed Kemi Oyl
along her scalp while she purred *Yes, Thank you, Rachel-face.*
Smoothed thick cream & pulled compression socks
on bony feet we once teased her about.
(My brother gave Evan, the funeral director,
a blanket to keep my mother's feet warm
while I fretted about the type of shoes
our mother should wear inside of her
casket.) But before I accepted her
dying, which would be true
five months later, I kept trying to write
my mother a strong beginning.
We slept on the floor of the waiting room.
We drank coffee & ate out of foil or boxes.

We took shifts, stepping in & out of hell.
We never abandoned her. We went out
& walked around Jefferson Hospital
looking for the right food to put some
weight on her smile. Her body was the only home
I cared about. I watched red & green lines on screens,
wrote out notes & dosages, walked down freakish
hallways after midnights. Bodies, at unrest. Bodies
snoring, groaning, farting, cursing, screaming
& sighing in yellow tunnels. Blank & courteous,
my uninsurable mind would come back to
the same idea: *my mother is going to live*
because *she is just going to live.*
& you know I would begin the list again,
revising the mercy of the God I knew.
I dreamt in the hideous chapel. Prayers
drying desperately on my lips. I'd rub balm
against my mother's mouth, hold the straw
while she barely sipped, shaking her
girlish head if the water wasn't cold
enough. Then the pain gripped us
too in the irritated drip beneath her
quiet voice. I would speak to her.
Look into brown eyes that I now see
whenever I look into rain.
Sometimes I'd hum alone in the middle
of the night. I didn't know who
I was trying to save anymore.
My mother was so close to us
I could almost reach her bad heart,
the tired organs stalling in her
body. I believed & believed
if I took more care with her life

there would be a god
who cared more than the god
who did not think
about our bodies, about the divine
grief of daughters,
about my mother, or the ache
in these stanzas, these too-thin
veins that still river
our lives in blood.

ARS POETICA

In the evenings, we watched *Jeopardy*.
Wore surgical masks once she got sick.
Before that my mother often sent me to the store
for cigarettes. Packs of Salem Lights.
Take somebody with you she'd tell me
but I didn't listen. Only wanted to get back
to the book on my lap. Didn't want to share
the change with my siblings so I could buy
chips, grape Now & Laters, & red Huggie
barrels for myself. We microwaved
fluid in clear bags for her "exchanges."
That's what the word meant
when my mother connected the plastic tube
from her stomach to a piss-colored sack
of peritoneal fluid. Normal dialysis was too much.
Before all that my mother smoked. We would
drive late to liquor stores for boxed wine. Six packs.
Then she got on the phone with her friends, kept
her feet up on an open oven to stay warm, laughed
the laughs she needed to help her get by, get up
the next day, & mother us all over again.
At night she did what she wanted. Cursed
so sublimely I learned to hear it as poetry
(unless I was the beloved of her ode).
Before she got sick, around the age I am now,
she wore her hair short, dyed a color
I can only describe as "Fuck You" red. She'd smoke
wearing her pearls. Ask me about school
& What Did I Want To Be
because she figured it'd likely cost her a lot of money.

Sometimes she'd say *Rachel-face, I need you to go to the store.*
I'd put down my book or the knife on the cutting board.
I'd walk alone in ugly jeans & Coke-bottle glasses
to Concord Deli, thinking about whether I could be
a writer someday. If I would ever learn to smoke, curse,
& two-step against a hot stove while my children grew up
like books or strangers under my own roof. What would it cost me
to make up true stories? How much would I have to save
of my life to pay my own way? When my neighbor said *Hey Beautiful*
I was thinking of how to get out of doing the dishes. Besides,
I didn't reply because I wasn't beautiful. But his friend braked
hard, barking like a dog, while he jumped from the car & ran over
our shadows on the sidewalk. *Hey Bitch*, he said
& flicked his cigarette down where we were both
dark as asphalt. The memory shivered in the skillet
the way the onions did when I came back into the kitchen
with my mother's cigarettes. Put the book away
& picked up the knife.

CATHEDRAL OF THE SNAKE & SAINT

(for the poet Maya Angelou, who died two months before my mother)

Riverside Church in September one sunlit morning we gathered
to sing farewell to our beloved sister, poet, our warrior
from St. Louis, raised in Stamps by her grandmother.
I thought it was too soon for me to go into a church. I wasn't civil
yet. I still crossed the street whenever I saw a sanctuary.
Then I would find myself, as if I had no luck, no choice,
crossing back again, searching for a quarter in my purse.
I would always light a candle. Couldn't bear to think
that if I didn't say a prayer what my dead mother might say or do.
& what she would have done that day (laughed & laughed)
to see her snake-headed daughter clapping & crying too loud,
carrying on like I was homeless, with a grief
only a god could wrestle from my soul. I shivered
on the white teeth of the holy spirit. Our people screamed
her name in the hollows. *Maya Maya Maya*
while she rose up & flew with wings so wide I was cold
from the brilliant shade they made. Indolent black angel
risen from her cage. There was that. But the singing. The singing!
I was shouting so wild & sad when Guy spoke at the finale
that the zipper of my dress snapped. My back exposed
right down to the black waistband of my panties.
The man behind me made a noise. I sat down fast in the dress
I'd worn to my mother's funeral. My good black dress with its snakeskin
panel down the front. A dress of death appropriate yet not animal enough.
I found it a few minutes after I chose my mother's burial suit,
an ivory Calvin Klein jacket & skirt. Feather-grey camisole.
Remembered once my mother said *Nobody will give you the skin*
off their back but me. I'm always going to love you. Because I'm your Mother.
But that morning I died again in the pew. God against my skin.

My entire body published like an unfinished deed to something, someone
I no longer owned. Clothed in her own grief, my best friend
could not give me her jacket. Could not allow the eyes of summer
to glare at her soft brown arms. Could not protect me
from the beak of death that still had not had enough (of me).
I rushed to the back of Riverside Church & flattened myself
against a pillar of stone. Wondered what would happen
if, upon my belly, I began to hiss, with my mournful fangs.
Friends went by, hugging & smiling, after the tribute ended.
I could not move. Hugged nothing but stone. Too mad to cry.
Nothing between me & my God. Flesh, stone, immediate shame.
There went the great bright flock. Valerie Simpson, who tore it up
earlier while performing *I'm Every Woman*. There was Toni
waving in a fine straw hat. & Nikki Giovanni & Hillary Clinton
& Marie & Jenisha. Then me, barely me, there against the stone, pinned
like an empty black tube of skin. I almost stepped right out of
the dead dress & why not? The edge of my mother's casket pulled
again against the split silk. Everything ugly & sweet in me
exposed to the heavens. So funny I hoped Saint Maya would thank me
in her throaty chuckle, would hold me in her arms & promise
I Believe You Can Save Yourself.

HUNGER

Weeks after her death I came to the garden window
to marvel at sudden pale feathers catching, scattering
past the rainy glass. I looked for magic everywhere.
Signs from the afterlife that I was, indeed, distinct.
Beneath the talon of a red-tailed hawk a pigeon
moved briefly until it didn't. The hawk stripped
the common bird, piercing its thick neck. Beak probing body
until I could see the blood from where I stood inside.
This could happen, naturally enough, even in Brooklyn.
This could happen whether or not my mother was dead.
I didn't eat for weeks because it felt wrong to want bread & milk.
The hawk's face turning red, beautiful as it plucked & picked
its silver-white prey apart. It wasn't magic, but hungrily, I watched.
As if I didn't know memory could devour corpses
caught alive in midair. I opened the window,
knelt on the fire escape. I was the prey
& hawk. This was finally myself swallowing
those small, common parts of me. Tearing all of that away
into strips, my breast open to the bone. I saw myself
torn apart, tearing & tearing at the beautiful face,
the throat beneath my claw. My grieving face red
with being exactly what I knew myself to be.

HEART OF DARKNESS

Years ago I went to Noho Star
with some poets & Cecil Taylor.
Noho Star is closed now
& Cecil died yesterday. I walked
to Union Square & watched black
men playing chess. Rubbing their jaws
while the afternoon light poured
down the gentle rooks of their fingers
hanging above a queen or pawn.
Cecil Taylor sat across the table
from me. Wearing leather gym
shorts, rainbow-striped knee socks,
a fringe vest, & a face so musical
I could hear the notes blunting
& banging as he low-laughed & looked
like a lion who had bitten off
the ancient secret of a soft roar. I
liked him right away. Said yes when
he asked me if I would share
a dessert with him. I in an ivory
dress that was vintage, the kind
my mother would have worn,
with chiffon sleeves—the shining
air made the loose dress
cling to me. The way a special
music clung to Cecil Taylor,
followed the radical swing &
swag of his voice. *Do you want*
to have the Heart of Darkness

together, he said. *That looks*
sweet enough. I remembered
later when we stood on the sidewalk,
sugar & poetry in us. Heat
coming off the summer night in the city
always made me feel I could
never leave New York. He kissed
my cheeks. Said he had been fooled.
I didn't think they made women
like you anymore. Tipped his cowboy hat
& took off his sunglasses. My god,
in the dark his eyes burned so clear
& wild I thought the sun was out, roaring
through our hearts like a song
daring its hunter to aim.

ILLUSION

Waiting inside of the night,
I could make out the mound
& my mother's eyes, the blank embrace
of innocence when she returned
from the other side of the light
where everything wept
as it was loved & forgotten.
It's your turn, it's always
your turn,
the night says.

CERTIFIED

We had to prove everything.
My mother was born Tuesday,
August 31, 1954. On that weekday
inside the womb of a minute
she burst from another woman's life,
gasping her first breath of light
in a demolished room
at D.C. General Hospital,
which no longer exists in the extraordinary ways
my mother no longer exists. I hope she was
swaddled tightly at her birth. Shit
& ~~music~~ mucus wiped away
from her small brown face.
Her story, gossamer—almost unobserved—
streamed like a tender, moonlit kite
from a spider's belly. Inside her I was
already waiting. My mother went to school.
Fainted in class from hunger. Her little brother
Pasqual drowned in a D.C. city pool. My mother
walked, like other poor black girls,
to class with cardboard for the soles of her shoes.
Fought rats for white bread in the kitchen cupboard.
Her family's living room furniture on the sidewalk.
Her mother dead at thirty-six from cervical cancer.
Which makes the velvet sack of red clots weary
in me. My future. My mother got her GED.
Decades later she'd have a college diploma.
For years she gave paper her paranoia, her respect,
her grudges. Whatever was written was law. Made history
liable even when it lied. Then paper wrapped around her

body, around her organs. Her medical files could fill
a school, a mansion. Insurance & charts. X-rays.
Letters from specialists. The results of tests
that would judge her impossible future *Impossible.*
So many referrals. So many prescriptions.
It was another language. A loosening hammock
of alphabets & symbols provoked her night & day. Insomnia
at her heels like the claws of a leopard. Spotted
& quickly at her throat before she could swallow.
Each diagnosis sustained a lie that she might make it.
At least get by. The donor forms, the miscellaneous
handwritten symptoms that stacked & scattered
like the savage tongues of Babel. I'd bring home homework
until she could no longer help me, could no longer make
sense of the equations. There were recipes she cooked.
Maps & illegible manuals of meds to keep her here with us.
Blood pressure, cholesterol, anti-rejection, vitamins
for endless deficiencies. Then the death certificate.
Multi-organ failure. July 28, 2014.
Time of death: 7:09 pm.
A piece of paper signed by a woman named Nathalie.
A simple statement of the body ceasing.
A cavity of boxes, a necessary form without breath.
We had to wait until the certificate got signed
by who & who & who to say
she would not come back.
Then I had these dreams
where I was writing at a desk.
The table made out of glass.
She'd come up & stand behind me,
sounding out the words.
When I looked down there was no paper.
Just her dead face trapped under the glass
casket that I inscribed with what

I was trying to remember.
When I turned to look over my shoulder
there was no body, no mother, no,
nothing but cobwebs of words.
Zombies twisted out of paper
holding their arms out
until I begged them, begged myself,
to let my mother *be*.

FATHER

Sometimes you tell us the story
about a time when you were young
& we were unborn. You followed other
laws then, being You & not a Father.
You were a police officer on the late beat,
thinking about your future, is how I imagine
you then. The story is that you saw a man dying
in the February snow. This was your work.
You saw a man dying alone in Washington's
snowfall. Your eyes fastened to the light
vapors rising in the last red gashes of
an innocent man's life. He had been robbed,
stabbed. You said the snow was stabbing
the night or was it music? Yes, Minnie
Riperton playing on all of the radios.
Sometimes you add more or less
to the memory. And what is memory
if not a bewitching math of error &
correction? You said you had never seen
a body die so quietly, so eerily, alone.
It is difficult to stand inside of the memory
of a man who will give life to me.
A man whose wounds will drift inside
of my birth. I would like to believe
that I loved you before I ever arrived
but maybe that is just the glass-eyed
poet in me or the daughter who clings
to the romance of remembrance, the labor
of stories & histories that precede
the raw material. You tell the story

of the dead man too often. Your eyes
go still as you look down at your hands
& clear your throat. You look down
at hands that once cupped my entire body
in one palm. Your first breathing daughter after
Mom's stillbirth. I remember the brittle leaf blowing
off the hook in my throat, whistling
itself into dust the first time I looked
at your new hands. You, my father, born again
in the word *widower*. Your vow removed
from your ring finger as you casually cut
a piece of meat on a plate. Your skin bare
as though there had never been a promise
to my mother, to me. "'Til death do us
part & she is dead," you said something
like that at the table in a restaurant
at a party for my brother's birthday.
I got up & walked away, dragging
a tantrum of screams that kicked
& slobbered tearfully inside my
windpipe. Within me a metallic ring
fell against forever—a womb
or grave—closing its dark eye in rest.
The man who wore that ring
is a memory now. The way
the snow is still melting
in my mind upon the dead man's
innocence.

MIRROR

I am not cruel, only truthful—
The eye of a little god, four-cornered.

   —SYLVIA PLATH

You immaculate bitch of glass, I'm doing all
the digging. Clods of blood & veins
I've never seen until you revealed to me
your mastery. You make no effort
while I turn away, dazzled. Your memory
as simple as a puddle. Like the moon or sun
or face that possesses me,
you won't leave.

I want you so ordinary.
I want you so sticky. Not like honey or strawberry bubble gum
or the thin cloud of joy that dries on my stomach & lips.
I said *sticky*. I want the sigh you make when sleep
is near, so close to your eyelids you smile & make a breezy sound
that is only yours as you step into a dream
where you fly & ride dragons. I am the dragon,
not the Last Dragon, but the one
to whom you'll surrender your divinity.
Lay your cheek against my scaly wings.
I want you plain. I want you bragging. I want you
naked as a tongue without a word. I want you
laughing. I want you joy. I want you wonder & wonderful.
The hips on every guitar. Copper tambourines
scoring your laughter. Don't ever learn how to stop
laughing. Laugh when you shouldn't. I like that
laughing best. I want you miracle. I want you possible
& foolish. What can't the heart love back
& rough so rough the muscles in us let go
& let you come into you. I want you tickled.
I want you shaking your head
like you can't believe this shit. I want you
dancing. Any kind of dance that takes you over
our ceiling of stars, over the commandment of my mouth,
over the blackening backs of mountains that have pushed through
the wide earth & ocean to see you sailing by.
You are rolling thigh then ass then waist then breast
then arms & shoulders. Your nerdy head is off!
You're in a circle & your good love keeps counting.
You good, yeah you good. Good good good & good.

I want you floating & swimming & finding yourself
so thrilled you pinch yourself, touch yourself
until you're screaming your own name
because you believe, like I believe, your name
is perfect. I want you rich like chocolate
with chocolate & chocolate & then some more
sugar. I want you sweet like two babies
with two puppies with two kittens with two
chocolate ice cream cones drooling down their cheeks.
That's sweet, right? Even when those hard nights & days
crawl under the hidden veil I have made for you,
even as your wings & bones promise you pain
& grief, remember what we know.
Remember what I've told you. I want you
drowning in paradise, whatever you remember
from the place we went to that one time.
& no matter how many moments
some god or death told us we had to leave
we said *Hell No.* When some fucked injustice
smiled & shot into the crowd & said
Y'all need to go back from where you came from.
Well, we stayed & lived. We danced &
remembered we were already arriving in love
through our mothers & fathers.
(Milton threw up his hands in defeat.
Said we didn't get it.) But the truth is
we didn't lose a thing. The paradise is
that we never left our homes. Instead,
we carried them around on our black hips
like a secret we already had all to ourselves.

NAME

In the brilliant beginning, I waited.
In the hot wake I watched how the word of her
rolled across the horizon as it was pulled
under the body that died. I was awake
all night after she died. Awake, terrible universe,
awake inside of my blood I could hear it,
the end of the daughter who could bleed
for no good reason. The first terrible morning & all,
all the windows were closed inside my waking.
The silence curdled my nostrils & veins. The air
dissolved our bridge of flesh. I get up from the shape I
once was. Death opens the white blinds in my brother's house.
The light is specific. It is the 29th morning of July.
Last night they dragged me howling from her
body in the room. The room had windows, a common
name—3315—in the cardiac wing. In the hospital room
I watched my mother rising, finally, from her battleship.
Now we meet in my body: I—
stare, day after day, into covered mirrors
while the good world sleeps
its aggrieved dream of living. Behind my eyes
a dead woman looks back at me with no trace
of recognition. I say *Mother* & my own mouth
opens & closes the air inside the window of my mouth
or keeps it out. The word feels so alive beneath
this house I hope these walls & flowers will not give
my grief a kind shelter.

There is only what we say we feel. For example: pain.
Or, *I am tired. When can I rest? What time should we get there?*
Sunlight & moonlight burn our brutal manners
of empathy. Beyond the song we hoped would go on
because we needed it for ourselves. Eternity has nothing
to do with us. Our seizures of imagination provide us
with language, civilization. Introductions of the super ego.
The condition of grief is an empty storefront. The paper of the map
but not the map itself, not the wishful drawings that promise
that we will be neither lost nor discovered. Not the sea, not the sweat,
not the tears that soak the paper, blur the destination where
only the foundation of home reveals there was ever a home.
Is that also the truth of our names? A way to announce we are a home?
O, strip mall of blood. O, neglected yard. O, mansion of marble &
gold with aisles of armored knights. Our minds tilt upon the closed
eyelids of justice, of freedom. Who names the body
of the oppressor when I say the oppressor does not exist if
I have murdered his name & burned his house down?

What do I call You?
The thoughtless look in the eyes of
the dying man or animal. A fading beast
that growls or giggles
while the living hold fast
in selfish terror: *Let Go of Me.*

Also, Death moved like honey, slowly unmaking
the flower of my mother while she died. While she died
the sun was setting. Her time of death:

                           7:09 pm

                         She looked at Nothing I could

see.
I only hoped it was better: the brightest
Nothing she saw at last.

                       •

This hemisphere of grief has bid me walk a motherless road.
The bulbs of the horse lamps are battered by darkness
on every side. Without milk or blood, we stutter against distance.
Because of what the rain did last spring to anything I dreamt. Then the sun:
    afterward:
        A woman coaxed seven stained figs, one by one,
        from the unloved tongue
        between my legs. "We're animals,"
        she said. "And you need a feeding."

                       •

I am too awake, too beautiful sometimes
    for my business on this page. Shadowboxed by the alphabet's
    decent, black knuckles, I am too free.

Don't tell me what time is too dull & shortsighted
to heal. Don't you ever heal me.

Don't say that love will help me now:

The windows in my brother's house were closed.
How would my mother find us again with so much starlight?
How would I know who the wind was &
was it any different than when my mother was
breathing her name across the sky?

.

At the hospital, I closed her eyes with the tips of my fingers.

.

In summertime winter dripped
from my mother's bones. One day I'll meet her
with my stones & flowers. I'll have her home-training
& my belly laughter. I'll use my hammer to shatter
our truth & our lies. I'll offer my difficult love, my radical
grammar of pictures. I'll carry our bones.

I'll wear a soft hide of fur. Four-legged,
she'll look at me, bear our deaths
with the mercy that was shown to us
when she smiled goodbye.

All that mattered to me
was that I could be sure my mother had enough
peace. When she died her eyes remained
half-opened. Looking out the way she always
had looked at nothing before she went to sleep.
Her eyes now heavy with the universe: a new body
so strong & pure
it burst her veins.

Two years later in Brooklyn I am getting my eyes
checked. I have good eyes today. But there were
whole years I couldn't see. Sometimes, it was love or art
that left me crawling in a tunnel. Sometimes I saw
choke-chains slither with my own hatred. The desire
to will myself blind so that I could not see
my face except in shadow.

Right now a woman is on the phone
near me in the place where sight is repaired
& restored. This attention to vision, the frames
arranged like invisible faces watching us.

"You don't have to be brave
in the face of pain," she said to a stranger,
some silent sufferer calling
on the other end. Some wound, someone

listening. What did she mean when she hung
up the phone then turned to me to ask what
time it was? Did she mean suffering?

I'm going to take my break. I can't stand this
place. The way they work you like we got all the time
in the damn world.

Why hadn't anyone told her that pain & time
possessed the same anatomy, the same
useless hands?

.

A dead woman is always looking at a book
or a mirror or at the sea. She is looking for edges
where her face dissolves into depths. Memories she
licks & places her fingers inside so they won't fall
apart: it's precise & wonderful: the beeswax melting
over her nipples & her mind. What is preserved
in grief cannot be golden, cannot be burned down
to make anything but a story or idol. Yes, it is true:

I am lifting my mother towards the glittering gods
who lash the rivers of my dreams with light.

Yes—

I am opening myself for the black-horned galaxies
where the soul hides, endangered by its unknown gibbering
alphabet. There was music I only knew by the ringing of

my teeth. And when pleasure sang me open & hot
I offered my cries to all dead mothers, so bruised
& beloved by their gods.

But now, now what does ripeness have to do
with me anymore?

.

Afterwards, emptied & emptying,
I stood near a window & looked down at the naked world
my mother loved so much she smiled as she was
leaving the empire of her body. Even now she is
still making me. What love cannot colonize
it burns. My mother's maiden name
is a verb: Pray.

.

I name you 'Mother'—

> The dead woman in the dark
> tells me a story so wide
> the loneliness falls away. I'm left
> with the toil of pleasure,
> the cry of
> other animals eating more bones
> than the earth herself
> can swallow.

Sometimes I have a name,
which means there is still a desire in me
to ask *Why?*

·

The galaxy has told me there is nothing
but matter to destroy itself, make itself, create
the hope we do not end.

daughter: lyric: landscape

good death

ELEGY, SURROUNDED BY SEVEN TREES

All Saints Cemetery, Wilmington, Delaware

Ordinary days deliver joy easily
again & I can't take it. If I could tell you
how her eyes laughed or describe
the rage of her suffering, I must
admit that lately my memories
are sometimes like a color
warping in my blue mind.

Metal abandoned in rain. My mother
will not move. Which is to say that
sometimes the true color of
her casket jumps from my head
like something burnt down
in the genesis of a struck flame.

Which is to say that I miss
the mind I had when I had
my mother. I own what is yet.

Which means I am already
holding my own absence
in faith. I still carry a faded slip of paper
where she once wrote a word
with a pencil & crossed it out.

From tree to tree, around her grave
I have walked, & turned back
if only to remind myself

that there are some kinds of
peace which will not be
moved. How awful to have such
wonder. The final way wonder itself
opened beneath my mother's face
at the last moment. As if she was

a small girl kneeling in a puddle
& looking at her face for the first time,
her fingers gripping the loud,
wet rim of the universe.

AUBADE TO LANGSTON

When the light wakes & finds again
the music of brooms in Mexico,
when daylight pulls our hands from grief,
& hearts cleaned raw with sawdust
& saltwater flood their dazzling vessels,
when the catfish in the river
raise their eyelids towards your face,
when sweetgrass bends in waves
across battlefields where sweat
& sugar marry, when we hear our people
wearing tongues fine with plain
greeting: *How You Doing, Good Morning,*
when I pour coffee & remember
my mother's love of buttered grits,
when the trains far away in memory
begin to turn their engine toward
a deep past of knowing,
when all I want to do is burn
my masks, when I see a woman
walking down the street holding her mind
like a leather belt, when I pluck a blues note
for my lazy shadow & cast its soul from my page,
when I see God's eyes looking up at black folks
flying between moonlight & museum,
when I see a good-looking people
who are my truest poetry,
when I pick up this pencil like a flute
& blow myself away from my death,
I listen to you again beneath the mercy
of a blue morning's grammar.

GOOD QUESTIONS

Who did you bleed for?

        The body required primary color. Iron. Salt. Sapphire.

Did you answer the void? Did you make any attempt to close the flesh?

        Yes, sometimes.

What did you give back after you gave everything up?

        Isn't that the same?

Answer the mother of your answers.

        Where *is* she? What has been done?

What are you trying to articulate?

        There were birds singing the very next morning. Why?

When did the final arrangements begin?

        At her birth. Inside of wet rock. When my birth began.
        At the red stones.

                      Did you already know?

        Birth & Experience had been established at once, you see.

                    You prayed before or after?

        Never stopped pulsing, the God—
        kept pushing through the earth of my mother
        like a hand in a dream.

                    What did you say?

        I knelt upon ashes, numb consonants. The swollen absence
        knifed my lips. I eat the fulfilled earth. I meant
        what I said about hunger.

                    Where were you?

        In my dream I heard her unlock the last gate. I was
        looking out from her unlit eyes, gasping. Black
        dogs of welcome. The call of the empty master.

                    Was it your blood or hers?

        The dark is possessive. The dark has always said Mine.

For months after her death I bled. I still bleed now
for no explicable reason. Honey, blood blood
blood. My grief was lush & sweet like the newlywed
bride that I was, buried in my mother's grave.
I knew too much about veils. I stared into the dark
eyes of my mother's new groom. Then I thought maybe
I would die too again in somebody's arms.

That's how much my life hurt. My hair fell out.
Kinky questions black on my pillow, I wore wigs.
My doctor spoke of mutiny, of my eggs, the starless issue
of impossible children. I stopped drinking, stopped playing
roulette with the world. I knew I no longer had extra time
to kill myself. I walked through open markets with nothing
in my cart. I was used to pushing my mother's heavy loads.
When I was a girl I watched her
press long fingers against fruit. Check for expiration
dates on packs of chicken thighs on sale. Chops.
Smoked bacon. Gallons of whole milk.

Despite the bleeding, the frank blood
I spill on this page, my verb tenses still
change all of the time. "I have a mother who."
"I had a mother who."
"My mother is—"
"Well, she was—"
"My mother loves
& liked to—"

What frightened me more
than the blood or eggs or beautiful, black
hair that fell in waves & curls
whenever I removed my shirt
or unzipped my coat (hair falling carefully
to the ground) was that

I couldn't read anything.

Behind the wheel of my car I stared at stop signs,
puzzled. Did I have to listen now? Did I have to
obey anymore? Nobody listened when I said *Mom
don't die. Please don't die.* Prayers dripped down
my red face. Caution made me bleed. The black
& yellow shapes made me think of bees.

Nobody walked across the street that way.

I went to my wailing wall of women whose
flesh & charms had written antic manuals, alphabets
of rage & love. There I prayed. I hummed
alone, half-bald. Being born alone again.

I could not trust such sentences of faith or fiction. Instead, I read
menus, tabloids, true crimes, prescriptions. Transcribed
simple miracles for my anxiety.

I could not taste life or honey.

But I could bleed.

MY RAPES

Years ago I wrote this poem, as a child, tracing
my finger across a stream in the dark. A silent deer
gazed up through the black water at the blood on my nails.
A teacher pulled his prize-winning teeth across the shoulders
of my poems. "I gave you a hard critique," he said,
then offered to save me from becoming
a terrible poet. "You have potential," he wrote
in looping letters. Years ago I was living this
very poem again, walking alone on the street
in ripped clothes. A woman I loved told me
to use a clear verb. "Was it actually Rape? Like Rape-Rape?"
Another time a writer urged me to repeat the word
to get my point across once I really knew
what had happened in the story
I was making up. "Because it sounds like she wanted
something she shouldn't have wanted," he said.
"Maybe you repeat the word a lot so that we readers
know it's interior versus what's really happening."
Many semesters a student has come to me with her poems
& her eyes & her typed-up evidence & between us
placed the formatted corpse of a memory that won't lie still.
I tell her to let it bleed out, let it scream, let it be her heart
until her brain can lead her to a jury of her peers, a new law,
a power that will pull her out of the water, out of the jaws of
the animal that used her. I tell myself I have told her the wrong
way to go & that we madwomen will all be lost inside the ovens
of fairy tales. We will be the possessed witch, the little girl
fattened or thinned to be eaten or sacrificed, we will be the evil
stepmother, the grandmother, or the beauty who lies

confined to dream in glass. Because someone, I promise her,
will look away when it is time to look at the truth
while someone else will not. Often I have done both
while standing in the night & morning of my mirrors
that ripple with the history I am making up. I remember
walking naked on a back road & recognizing the torso
of a deer or maybe it was Shakespeare's sister, the part of her
flesh that leapt from the attic, the disembodied
mind & heart ripping the spine of her own books apart.
Why will we try to praise a mutilated world & leave
our mutilated women in the margins to fend
for our worth beneath moonlit headstones?
I want to believe I am urging survival,
that I live the same impulse of the great poets
to praise suffering, to feel the merciful world shimmering
in spite of its injury, but women everywhere
face our executioners, however kind or coarse.
Women, women, we who are burned alive, blown apart
across red scars that ripple beneath the secret parts
of the earth we may never save. We who want to possess her
but refuse to listen to her voice, hot & enraged with torture.
What does she know as she kneels in her long fever?
My living father will read this poem & close his eyes
& maybe his heart will be afraid for me. Years ago
I promised my mother I would never speak a word
about my rapes. I would never tell the world
about my power until she was dead. Her eyes sealed &
having a choice now to listen to me or be a ghost
when I am saying the difficult thing. This poem is
for my mother who always said the difficult thing
& lived it. My mother who was quick to threaten her enemies
with death. She showed me how to follow my heart into hard places.

This is for the women who were my teachers who told me
to be safe & leave my rapes out of my poems,
who said, "I think I always knew this about you" or
"Now I understand why you're so difficult" or
"You seem more real to me since your mother died."
Once I remember my mother, yes, asking why
I listened to white girl shit. How could alternative music
hear a black cry like mine? So I searched for the standards
where a sad black girl could sing her story from her bones
without her own family closing the doors of their eyes.
I found Eleanora Fagan & more, their voices crying
but fighting back. I listened like the river. But why did I have to
choose between being a color & being a girl?
Why did I have to choose between being a writer
& being a death? I pull joy from the ledges of my mistakes,
pull the muse by her wrists through broken windows, use shards
of glass to cast rainbows, the birth of self-
respect quickening. Do you want to try me? I remember
when I tried to tell my mother about the rapes she asked me
what in the world had I been wearing & where had I gone
where a man could have that chance. "I've been in the world,
just like everybody else," I told her, which was a stupid thing
to say. The world came after me. Praise the woman
who wrote, "For most of history, Anonymous
was a woman." & for the silence of the author's mind
& those terrible voices that pulled her under
the Ouse River, & too, for the silence of a London oven
in 1963, & the humming of the engine-heart
in a solitary car in its Weston garage in the autumn of 1974.
& for the labor, the work of women's backs
bending to hold their brilliance against black thirst.
& for the women whose sunny headstones

will be neither visited nor mapped on any page. For the jury
of our letters & stories, for those whose hands
grow rich from knowing what was stolen
or revised & will not write aloud
our names. This terrible poem is for us,
we outlaw women who have taken off the silence
of our muzzles & armed our bones with stars,
we who leap from the attics we are burning down.

COLOR THEORY & PRAXIS (I)

To the White Artist Who Said Her Painting of Emmett Till
Was about a Conversation with His Mother

In paint you're still pulling him
out of the river. Still taking the skin
off (again) with a ~~bullet~~ brush. Here is the head
his mother stared at, staring back
at your broken colors. Bruise as palette, as figure.
See, the angle isn't even dead. The day
before America elected 45 I walked through
a vast museum, starting in the pit
of a slave ship. Choking there in the dark,
I couldn't breathe upon those iron shackles
for an infant whose mother might have
held him to her heart as she leapt into the sea.
Don't tell me about a white woman's master-
piece: the tender wolf-whistle lying
atop black men's graves. I went to another exhibit
but I had to sit down. On a bench in front of Emmett
Till's first casket. His mother's voice clear
& strong in a video. A narrative. The black
woman, alive, next to me, couldn't stop crying.
~~A mug shot photograph of~~ the boy's face
taped to the museum glass where the body
is there (always). Who would dare
paint it? Pluck the wound into cubes,
globs of cadmium & lashes of umber? What
artist could stand for days in front of
our brother's body? When they write
about destroying the painting, all I
can think of is who must remember

our devastation if not us? A color-
by-number. For sixty million. The artist says
                      she'll never sell him ~~the painting~~
~~down the river.~~ Imagine what it would take
to paint millions of broken black bones that way?
Dare she think she owns us too: the still-life my people
are still dying for?

ABOUT THE FLOWERS

There are calla lilies, long upon the mute lid
of my mother's name. A smudge of summer
beneath the scent of what is dead in me.

There is magnolia somewhere all year long.
The beginning of death leaves a strong taste
I must remember I already know.

I keep trying to stay near her death.
I must stop gathering the stems & dust &
the nights I walked through my mind
holding a camera against the darkening.

In every window some cloud, some sky,
some reflection of happiness
streaked bitterly with beauty & ache.

We break mirrors inside of each other
to see again. Lord, trees & flowers & joy
are too simple again. I keep trying to hear

how the roses shivered
as they fell inside of the soft throat
of our farewell.

HUSBAND

Forgive the hours you waited in our ruin
of happiness. We always knew I was wild, wrecked
with wonder I could not bring into our house
without printing our floor with blood. My past
swung on a cord from the ceiling. The glare of light
in me crashed against the walls like stacked plates.
Forgive the moment you came through the door
& found me for the hundredth time in a heap
of light next to the clump of my skin. Forgive
the fun we tried to have. Forgive the hours &
hours we worked. Why did we work so hard for each other?
Believing that work would be enough. Days & nights
we walked through Brooklyn, our happy dog leashed
between our lonely shadows. Forgive me for being
a shadow for years. When I showed up
you were already someone else. Under a full moon
in Mexico we ate white cake. Hoped like waves.
Flowers in my hair. Lizards on the stones. Bouquet
we stashed in a suitcase then the refrigerator.
Forgive us for not knowing the faces of silence
that would make our voices strange, strained,
stranded in vicious loneliness, side by side
in bed. When my mother died I could not confess
I was neither a daughter nor a wife. How to tell you
I was merely nothing, a breeze or wave or word
blacked-out, gibbering against vows, ash, sand.
For six months we were newlyweds. I remember
my smiling mother in a long pink dress, fixing
the diamonds at my ears, dancing later in her body
that hadn't yet given up pleasure. Forgive how beautiful

we were at that collision of sea & moon & freedom.
Forgive me for the unborn children I couldn't have,
for the little girl in me you kept saving. A child
rocking the childhood where her stuffed grizzly bear
smiled in its broken rocking chair of nightmares. Forgive
our devastation & devotion. I told you farewell
because farewells were my favorite things.
But I hadn't lost you yet. Or her. I hadn't
lost anything yet that had lungs of its own.
I wished you love, wished for you a life
more faithful than this poem. I wish it for you yet,
my love. I wish you had not stood so closely
next to my mother's grave where I had disappeared.
Why did you follow me? Forgive me for giving you
a grave instead of a home. We should have framed
the ketubah right away.
For years I photographed myself
in a white dress. Terrified by my belief
that I might be a ghost. A barren veil. A figure
framed by my future & my past. Forgive
my estranged affair with the present. I'm consumed
with common tenses & my mother's visitations. My bride
a naked solitude without ornament. Forgive
the high, hard wall of our memory
where the bulb finally shattered.

GOOD DEEDS

Then think of every song of love hurled at you & yours.
Recall how battered you were by sheer understanding
so that you might surrender. Not her being gone
but everything else. The world insists
you return. You go along with the house rules,
what the passage of sunlight means, a warmth
that is bold enough to burn the world alive.
I say I can't remember how to be the same. I say
I can't pretend to be that woman, the world,
or the love song you left behind your eyes.
I say that I am beginning to understand
the way my friends sing alone inside of walls.

COLOR THEORY & PRAXIS (II)

To the Child of the White Artist Whose Mother
Said Her Painting of Emmett Till Was about a Conversation
with His Mother

Forgive me. Is that what your mother meant?
Was it shame or a sensation, *this could be mine,* my own
child dragged up from ole Dixie's depths? Some new art,
abstract & apologetic, a language could be conjured
in paint. You are walking into a store in 1955
& think you can expect that your child will
receive something different than the child
of the mother who could barely recognize
her own baby when they finished with his
body? It was her imagination & what is that?
Your mother has no intention of selling
it, she says. After all, a black boy's face is free speech
somewhere. Is that what your mother meant?
Or did she slip her art into another woman's
grief with new, long brushes & white canvas?
Child, did she tell you what it meant?
When I have to get up in the godless night
& trace my brother's name with a prayer.
Drag his death (again) through burnt syllables
until my own blood writes & writes & weeps
in the dry history. Did your mother mean
for me to hear Mamie Till's scream in the photograph
she painted? Mamie, black woman, monochrome
of her moan above the flower of her son's face? Child,
tell me, what color does your future have? &
what will my unborn children forgive
when they are asked to love you?

WHIPPING TREE

Laurel Grove Cemetery South, Savannah, Georgia, 2018

Where are the whips & hands
that risked their own history
to lash lessons of blood
upon black bodies roped
against these simple oaks?
The marks are too high
to touch now, the evidence too
grotesque to scab our wailing eyes.
I am trying to translate a word
that glows like a chain. It is nearly
God. The thick trees have grown tall
beyond their unbearable childhoods.

In the tree, I see which way the master
snapped his wrist, turned directions, changing
his mind when the body didn't scream loud
enough, when the eyes of the slave refused
to look away from the master she once nursed.

Were there days he tired from bringing the whip
across his thin freedom & did he throw his ugly work
to another man as he walked, tenderly,
to a house he dared to call his home?

      The south stands in the throat of a tree.

Truth is a scraped breath between glorious
brown limbs. How hard was it for them

to gather their blistered family into gentle arms
& keep singing to Jesus? I want what flesh
they hymned. Every flap of skin crying
& glowing red in faith.

      I can't look away from these unbroken trees.

I am aware that we are living in the middle
ring of terrorism. The trouble of scars
bleeding through new maps. The tree
trying, alone, to survive our dead
names in the stripped bark.

GOOD AMERICA, GOOD ACTS

Now imagine she's white.
        —*Jake Brigance, closing argument in the film* A Time to Kill

Imagine it's your daughter or your mother
or someone you're sure you never met before. Imagine
if you cared to begin with. Then begin with the picture
in your mind that will make her matter. Imagine
her pale breasts crushed against the earth
of this poem. Imagine the woman
on the Alabama floor saying *But I'm not doing anything to you*
& then you are doing something or nothing, perhaps
eating or ignoring her screams as police pray
their knees into her flesh. Now imagine she's black.
Imagine a cop's hungry threat made true: *I'm about to break your arm*
that's what I'm about to do. Imagine magnolia shaking
against the sticky walls of this poem. It's spring in the south.
Mute light washes the flat parking lot. Exposed lines
in the night. That way that America has never surrendered
exposing its lust for blood. How disordered the dream of
justice sings through ugly diner speakers, grubby fingers
fingering the knob of her breast. Imagine her
choking on the threat that never existed until an employee
called 911. Imagine if a woman were to exist at all. Her beauty
pulled down to her waist & trembling. Imagine America
is a woman & you can't believe women yet.
Her cheek pressed against a floor littered
with torn napkins, ketchup & the imprints of work boots,
artificial syrup, filth. Perhaps your phone is ringing
but with closed eyes you almost see the white woman again
on the floor. Perhaps you think you should call someone
for help. You sit at a table staring out of the window

at some flickering taillight of justice, a shadow
you have seen all your life. You aren't doing anything anymore.
You've never done anything. Not you, not your country.
Everything that happened was long ago.
You pick up your knife & lower your voice
beneath her cries. You don't stand up & say you won't
watch them do what they have done. Dragged her back
behind the slave cabins or into the forest or master's bedroom.
This property of memory so necessary you don't flinch
while you swallow waffles. *She's not white now so—*
                    But imagine what you deserve. What have you done?
A woman bears a threat if she exists. Under arrest, she feeds you.
Imagine this poem against your temple, pressing
its hiss against your head. Yes,
America, you've done just about enough.

MYTH

Here is the worship. Here is the wound.
Here is the housework of our sad mothers, again
& again. Where is the world where a black boy is
not a wound shivering in his blue skin
beneath a bullet's moonlight?

A mustard seed of fear soaked in blood. In the literature
of blood the black face gasps for air. No, in the jury
of blood the black boy's face merely insists
it is a face to begin with.

Where is the story that began in the ditch
of a religion, in the hull of a need
so sick & swollen it floated my people
across its terrible waves?

Who wrote the end of my brothers' lives
in blood against the night sky, against the psalm
of bullets riven through our broken hearts?

We are dying. We are dying. We are dying.
We are dying in the name of a love
so evil it can't kill us quickly enough.

What do you believe?

Here is the faith I never wanted.
Here is a black child who looks like night
like red dirt like Easter morning. A black boy
who will not rise again when bullets spin away
from the crypt some cop has made of his body.

Seven days after my mother died
America aimed her myth
at Mike Brown.
Her grave was still new
when I went back to be sure
she was really there. I whispered
his name against the barrel of August
that shot through the blue clouds.

America shot Mike Brown
& I can't be sorry anymore
because I'm too angry, too tired,
too alive
to let their good myth put its hands
on me & mine.

In nightmares my mother & I stand
in the middle of the street, trying to rewind
the blood before it leaves
his body. Six times, six
sonnets of bullets. Why is the need
so deep & dusty? A boy prays facedown
in the street with no prayer. Who is god
to god?

Four hours they left a black boy
uncovered in his own death. Sleepless,
I could not stop seeing
my mother cradling Mike Brown
in her arms. She loved black children
more than anything.

Why is the need something
America is pretending not to know?

We know what we know.

WHO BY FIRE

And who shall I say is calling?

—LEONARD COHEN

Leonard, can I call on you again
in the night? The stars say I am to burn.
My friends say I'm not a true Sagittarius,
after all. I mix it up. Sometimes I prefer smoke
to flame, hoof to sole, arrow to reason. My mind opens
its hostile constellations & the sky of my skull
flickers wetly to black. Leonard, could you stand
how the light begged you to laugh in the dark? Did you
ever try to love a woman while standing up? I saw you
only once in flesh. On your knees, singing, the microphone
of your heart between your long hands. The shadow of
a blade-black hat holding you apart, above the lover
you tasted behind closed eyes. Whenever I listen to you
I can't help but hurt in grace. I want to say
Hallelujah again & again. I want to believe
my voice is a famous road or tower. Tell me:
where are the miracles now, Leonard? Do I believe
my dead mother's voice is a young cry
in the ground like a root? Is the end of grief
a tongue rolling over its own noise
to drink from a clear spring? What, darling,
about longing? How do I answer
these uninvited guests? Speech, love,
suffering, time & hunger. I wanted nothing
for years after her death. But now?
Well, I am some breed of music
singeing the wires. A flame returning
the anguish of a stranger who, by need,

holds my attention in the mirror.
Leonard, isn't language a lonely slip?
Or is it a drug so distinct it tames
our tongues with faith, so that God's
voice won't fall apart in a mutter? Black
diamond in the gutter, gorgeous flash of
clarity lost in the veins. Leonard, tell me
if I should ever answer the hush of my unlit
matchsticks in this endless wintering.
Or, if from need, I must strike & strike.

ANOTHER AGE

Last Dance of Suicide

This is the last day you will ever see me want to die.
Today is the last time I will consider a bridge, a bullet,
a train, or leather belt. A bottle of winter. Let this be the last day
sorrow will lend me her black dress
with its high side slit & tell me
       I am nothing
but jazz, smoke & sequin. Let this be the last day
I'll kiss sorrow with my tongue & promise her
       I've never cheated.
I glittered & glittered while she wasn't looking.
I couldn't help it.
       How did you sweet-talk your shotgun
into my mouth? Coming into my house
each night on your blue knees, crying *Baby, baby, baby*
like you knew me by a natural name.
       How can a fool survive a fool?
This is some new song of leather. These is bloody shoes.
I'll dance on my grave but never sleep there.
And your lonely music? You heard me begging
for our song to stop. Now, dear death,
I own my masters & my slaves.
The rights I've earned by blood & bruise.
The only blues is that I've left you for good.
How did I think I could speak of love
for myself while you cut the tongues out
of my own poems? Yes god yes
of course my life is mine

but who owns this singing if not
love? Let every scar welcome me
as I fly through the door of my flesh.
Beware, Suicide, whoever says
you & I are each other's
business.

GOOD FOOD

She didn't share her forks or spoons with us.
Nobody could drink from the same glass.
Get your own thing, she used to say.
My mother's table was clear & direct.

I miss her macaroni & cheese.
She made it the way black people make it.
& don't add all that other shit up in it that makes it
all mixed-up with some Indian in it.
I mean I miss her barbecue ribs.
I miss her potato salad. She had these deviled eggs
that were so wicked I couldn't say no.
& I don't even fuck with
deviled eggs like that.

She could take a piece of bread, a pinch of
salt, some olive oil, some whatever she didn't have,
& I'd find myself shiny & astonished
at how she taught herself to share
her impulsive feasts.

In the summer we'd gather around bushels of
blue crabs, baptized in beer, butter & Old Bay.
Ate the legs & the body, every part except
the lungs. She'd pull meat from shell & show me
how to feed myself. She liked sweet watermelon
in summer. Jesus, the way she would say *Sweet*
as though it was her first slice ever. I would stand
nearby, half-hiding, just to hear her say it
softly to herself.

Tell herself *Sweet, sweet, sweet.*

She made us scrapple & scrambled eggs
with cheese, potatoes, gravy & biscuits. *Scratch,
make it from scratch.* She taught me how to
roll my fingers, pull artichokes apart
until I reached the heart. Pound meat to soften
the flesh. How to make a sincere roux. Pull veins
out of shrimp. Shuck corn. Fry chicken legs
without getting hurt.

She could chase hunger away
like she was playing music by ear. There was an art,
an imagination with its steel lid off
so we could look in & down at something
she was giving back to us, all
put together to make, to improve
in our own way.

She was kind & hard
like fresh Red Delicious apples she chewed to core.
Yes, there were rules in her kitchen.
But I thought she was always going to be
there (until she wasn't).

Teaching us how to eat & to cook. Teaching us
how to clean up after our own messes. Telling
us not to lick a spoon & put it back
into the same pot of sauce. *Only white folks
did that* though I know now that isn't true.

I really don't want you to think there's a lesson
simmering somewhere in this poem.
Because this poem is about Delight,
missing that Delight but remembering
& remembering how to make it—Delight—
from scratch.

Please say in the afterlife you've given my mother something to do.
This talk of rest & peace would make her chuckle. Say *Yeah Right,*
if it isn't one thing in this life it's the next. So maybe death isn't one thing
except that death is, only saying everything once with a raised voice.
My mother got up every time she almost died & said
she had too much work to do. Somebody's last nerves somewhere
would miss her. Now, say that I will regret the years already
ahead of me. No kin-voice insisting, *I Remember Her Name. Do you*
Remember? My father forgets people's names all the time. But when he speaks
of his wife I see her without warning. The edges of her painted
fingernails & slender feet, disappearing. Fading like borders of poems
I first tried to write before I realized I could barely stand poetry
or save my mother's life. I don't know what my work is anymore,
except that the pressure of her fingertips appears in me like grammar.
How can I avoid embalming her twice by alphabet?
She, who used her hands to work, used her hands to cup her voice
when she couldn't speak. I was told that she pointed out
these words on a sheet of paper at the hospital: *I Want to Speak.*
But she couldn't then. Her voice in a tube. Her hands mute
upon white sheets. From life, she went on, loving us.
Her fingertips still touching our faces in good dreams
like Baby Suggs in the safe, bright woods, her black arms
outstretched good above the dust & dignity we are. Begging us
to raise our hands & heads high into the names the water
remembers. Our voice is the craft & laughter of beloved
children who call out yet for home, who live against the vanity
of suffering. We must be our own work. Our own true
sermon of excellent dust. Our greatest labor.

GOOD NIGHT

Threading the silver crust
of a nightmare with stars, I stitch
& pull my mother's name
through white stones that do not burn
in the riverbed of blood
beneath my tongue. The moon
is a knuckle, the crown of a nightly fist
pressed against my mouth. Tears
pour from my mouth. In absentia
someone votes for my life.

The night climbs my spine. My head
wrecked with involuntary stars.
May sorrow carry the good news
to every door
the body has marked
with blood.

Our visits go on inside
my skin, existing like the light
of planets whose extinction we have
yet to memorize. How do I remember
which forever is my mother's truth?

Her god bursts like rain
behind the earth's skull.
In water, our alphabet
sinks &

our arms, bare as ghosts,
drift

like thin ships of brown paper. Love persists
within my gold bones. I kneel
in the hull of memory.

My flesh is a syntax of dark grammar
sunken beneath my tongue.

For years & years you had her, I say
with blame.

Squealing & indigo, I take
my mother's words again.
Examine the fontanelles
of syllables, pressing
& striking
the echoes of her voice
until I scream & shriek
inside the lonely gauze
of my rebirth.

Newborn with sorrow,
I can see the shining
veins
we share when the world
leaves every face &
surface beatified
with suffering.

Tell me, I say.

I can't remember the thunder
that cracked my head
into stardust
above the hospital bed.

Tonight, my mother gets up
from her own silence
to tell me she believes
that we were all
the living she ever
wanted to say.

AS

until the day that you are me and I am you
—STEVIE WONDER

I flew to you   over darkening blue   waves & sky

I did not arrive in time   faith   snapped like a tongue

Mountain too low   bridge washed out   I'm numb

                              Beautiful Mother

   I never dreamed you'd leave in summer

Your gentle hand   in mine   your life

the antic bow   I shoulder I quiver I remember   Dahomey

      The new lurid scent

                  of a world

without you   shock & trouble   O my Mother

      I never dreamed you'd leave in summer

I flew from the roofs crying your name

                        come back come back come back

Without your shield   my arrows   returned to my heart

                              on my own command

Flung myself   into moonlit fires & silent days   ever after

                    I thought you would stay

O Mother   whose love swept over me   whose death

holds firm &   as I slip   sink into an afterlife

where ordinary life   ordinary injury

is merely the undertow   the sigh of

missing your

            smile   Held bravely as your last soft breath

You at last &

                    Why didn't you stay?

O Mother   without suffering without pain   O Mother

with beauty & mercy & dust   Oh my god *dust*

Mercy   leave   my Mother   to her   heaven

winter   autumn   spring   Leave my Mother

the dignity   of what   the earth   insists

I must say & say & say   kneeling upon a song

                              I never dreamed you'd leave in summer

inside the hot dust & blood & flower crumbling   a song

you lived & sang back & back to me:

                        love you love you love you love you love you

GOOD MOTHER

Praise the woman who took me in her arms &
wouldn't let go of me. We sank to the floor
in the middle of the aisle in Rite Aid.
It was a late morning & I walked slowly,
furious that spring could still be so wonderful.
Magnolia tempted me to forget about my mother
for a few minutes. I stared at a Brooklyn blue sky
through branches clasping pear blossoms.
The limbs shook in sunlight. My eyes adjusted
when I went into the pharmacy & realized
everywhere I looked the world announced
it would soon be Mother's Day. Something
ripped itself out of me. A howl so wide
I thought I would burst. The woman near the counter
understood right away the way my mother
once understood I had been born in a specific sadness.
The woman did not say she was a mother but I knew it.
She put her arms around me & waved away the cashiers,
the security guard who repeated *Ma'am, Ma'am?*
A stranger rocked me in her arms, so much kindness
as we fell over & crashed against a row of votive candles.
She didn't say it would be okay. She didn't ask me
what was wrong. But her arms put me in a vicious prayer.
I almost bit her, almost pushed her away.
We held on. We held on & praised the nameless thing
that makes us what we think we aren't strong enough
to know. She knew. She didn't let go of me.
Praise the woman who didn't wipe my snot from her shirt,
my tears from her collarbone, who did not tell me to
pull myself together while everything inside me dropped.

Crushed bones. Blossoms pushing through my mouth—
a word: *Mom Mom Mom.* This broken birdsong of mine
with no bird, no wing, no way to fly back through time.
Praise the woman who did not leave me
like something suddenly dead on the sidewalk
with a breeze blowing over its face.
Praise the woman who smelled like fabric softener
& coffee & the good things I must believe I am too.
Praise the mothers who walk slowly through the world,
bringing children into themselves, burying children sometimes
before themselves, & who defend something harder
than innocence. Praise the guts & grace of mothers.
Praise their exhaustion & their good work. Praise their wit,
their wonderful ways of listening to the world fall
asleep against its clean pillow. For the woman
who knelt with me in an ugly heap in the middle of
Rite Aid on an unbearable spring day,
who helped me buy a Mother's Day card
for my dead mother, who knew better than to say
I'd be just fine, for you I lift my arms each spring
& wish you a kindness so fantastic I sometimes feel
I'm in midair, the shadow of my wings clapping in joy
above your children who must love you.

CHOSEN FAMILY

When you find your people you'll still look over your shoulder sometimes
to see if you're being followed. You're hoping one or two people you don't
know will want to see where you're going. When you find your people
they won't ask you where you came from because they'll already know
& if they don't they'll be busy putting good food on your plate & asking you
if you're hungry or broke. When you find your people they'll tell you
to use any bathroom you want, marry anybody you want, work side-by-side
for long hours with full wages without any fear of being harmed.
When you find your people they'll throw their star to you, offer you
their love song & say you need to *listen to this dance & shine with us*
whether or not you know all the steps. When you find your people
they'll say *Do You Remember* & you'll say *Yes* until you remember together
the different ways the whole thing happened. When you find your people
they'll say wear whatever you want, wear the tightest dress, wear your hot pants,
your fishnets, your damn birthday suit. They'll say we love your black skin
& drag & fat & natural hair & we love you from your roots so please just live
& don't let anybody kill you or tell you they've killed you & you're just fine
the dead way you are. When you find your people don't leave them
& don't let them off the hook when they are in the wrong.
When they are trying to take themselves out of the world
lay your hands on them & call them yours & yours & yours.
When you find your people be sure you've been preparing
your difficult heart by loving yourself, & what you pretend you don't know
you actually do, so that when you see your kin smiling into your eyes, the soft
or tough flags of their hands covering yours in a truth so light & fierce,
you see you all have been midair for some time, & could go higher,
& burn some shit up, if you remembered what else is good,
everywhere & everywhere you look.

Of words placed in their best black clothes. Of that darkness full.
Of my mother's laughter, forged of great dust
   that spilled its golden light into her tomb.
Of the copper wreath carved upon her copper vault.
   God & Mother, I must speak to you.
   I must say: *It is good. Our death.*
Of the ivory city—bones like trumpets—
   blowing my mother away from me in song.
Of the city again where doves & vultures welcome my mother's life.
Of the road between her dates—a short slash—
   a bridge ends in oblivion. (Mother, you never end.)
Of the pronunciation of sorrow, forever mine, each astonishing summer.
Of the snake who suffered our story of knowledge & shame.
Of the afterlife & its downpour of ordinary rites.
Of the ordinary rites I enact in my broken thoughts.
Of my fever waving its anguish until the match goes out in disbelief.
Of Michael Brown bleeding without mercy
   beneath the concrete roof of God.
   Of God, God, & God.
Of the peace & suffering black people have been promised.
Of the clean, white clothes I gave my mother's undertaker.
   Here are the stockings, I said, not knowing
whether they would match my mother's skin or death.
Of the poems I've been trying to write. *Die*, I say.
   Go elsewhere for songs.
Of the food & the appetite.
Of my father's shoulders in a black suit.
Of the downpour against sunlight. The world, in friendship, returns my tears.
Of the wildest animals who charge at me with their horns
   when I offer my pentameter of ribs.

Of my mother's visitations. Of the messages I have missed.
Of the hot comb I cradled on my knees in the bathroom.
Of the brutal gospel of hair, untouched toothbrush, clothes
        in closets with sale tags.
Of dreams where my teeth scatter like maple leaves.
Of what I will never remember. There is no end of remembering.
Of the rain that makes my howls float like empty bottles of glass.
Of the dreams where my hot, white clothes grow flames.
Of what I will remember remembering about love.
Of the neon-colored nail polish on my mother's hand
        I held at her deathbed.
Of what I hated to ask the night & gods.
Of my knees that remember the orange mud
        before the grass grew back on her grave.
Of the strange, concerned question poured like sulfur
        over my side where I was trying to leave my skin.
Of it being over, again & again. Of it beginning.
        They asked me was it a Good Death, was it
        a Good Death? Was there *peace* for all of us? *Why*
        should I want *peace* instead of my Mother?
Of the mothers who have always known the ache of the earth
        while holding children in their wombs—*Why*
        wasn't I told you'd leave me?
Now I walk into the sea with my jewel of anguish
& shake my mothers, these shining human flowers,
        from my bald, newborn skull.

notes

"Chronology" is an ekphrastic poem that concentrates its energy in various works from the Alberto Burri exhibition, *The Trauma of Painting*, at the Guggenheim Museum in 2015.

"Arch of Hysteria, or, The Spider-Mother Becomes a Woman" is dedicated to the late artist Louise Bourgeois, whose courage, work, and life helped and challenged me to trust and to value my inner life and intuition.

"Ars Poetica" cites a procedure, related to renal failure, called peritoneal dialysis. I use the word "stomach" in my poem because as a child that's what it looked like to me. I am aware that the actual process does not use the stomach as a filter but rather the lining of the abdomen to filter waste from the blood, and that this process can differ between patients.

"Heart of Darkness" is dedicated to Cecil Taylor.

"Illusion" is dedicated to Nick Flynn.

"Aubade to Langston" is for Chi and Rickey. For those days and hours in Mississippi, forever will you be my family.

In "My Rapes," the phrase "try to praise a mutilated world" is taken from Adam Zagajewski's wonderful poem "Try to Praise the Mutilated World."

The poem "Good America, Good Acts" was written for Chikesia Clemons.

It contains the final line used to win the legal case that the actor Matthew McConaughey, playing the fictional character Jake Brigance, is arguing in the film adaptation of John Grisham's novel *A Time to Kill*.

On April 22, 2018, at a Waffle House in Saraland, Alabama, Chikesia Clemons, a 25-year-old mother, was violently restrained by three white male police officers who arrived at the restaurant after a white employee, who felt threatened by Clemons, called 911. Clemons's restraint was recorded, with footage of the white male officers using excessive force, which included choking her and threatening to break her arm while they forced her to the ground, exposing her breasts, during her arrest.

The poem "Another Age" contains a lyric from Cardi B's song *Bodak Yellow*, "These is bloody shoes."

The poem "Work" refers to Baby Suggs, who is a character in Toni Morrison's novel *Beloved*, and the "sermon" that Baby Suggs secretly gives at the Clearing.

The poem "As" uses two lyrics from Stevie Wonder's song "I Never Dreamed You'd Leave in Summer." Those two lines are *I never dreamed you'd leave in summer* and *Why didn't you stay?*

acknowledgments

Grateful acknowledgment is made to the editors of the following journals, who first published the following poems (and earlier versions of these poems):

Academy of American Poets, Poem-A-Day: "Name" (excerpt); "Elegy, Surrounded by Seven Trees"

American Poetry Review: "Myth" (as "Eurydice, Mississippi, 2014"); "Good Death"

BuzzFeed: "Color Theory & Praxis (I)" and "Color Theory & Praxis (II)" (as "To the White Artist Who Said Her Painting of Emmett Till Was about a Conversation with His Mother"; "To the Child of the White Artist Whose Mother Said Her Painting of Emmett Till Was about a Conversation with His Mother")

Cortland Review: "Good Night" (as "Elegy")

Guernica (introduction by Nick Flynn, 2014): "Illusion"

Gulf Coast: "Husband" (as "Good Husband")

Los Angeles Review of Books Quarterly Journal: "Chronology" (as "A Chronology of Scars"); "Good Questions"

New Daughters of Africa, edited by Margaret Busby (Myriad Editions, 2019): "Cathedral of the Snake & Saint"

The New Yorker: "Comedy"; "Heart of Darkness"

Paris Review: "Hunger"

The Progressive: "Chosen Family"

Southern Humanities Review: "Aubade to Langston"

The Southampton Review: "Paradise"

Tin House: "Volume"; "Good Mother"

Virginia Quarterly Review: "Seeing the Body"; "Arch of Hysteria"; "Belief"; "Ars Poetica"; "Certified"

·

The outpour of kindness, generosity, and love that was shown to me and to my family during our difficult loss is something I will never take for granted. I carry the gorgeous names of family (blood & chosen), aunts & uncles & cousins, sisters & brothers, friends & strangers, teachers & students, & fellow grievers wherever I go.

Here, aware that there are definitely individuals I may have overlooked (because I am fortunate to know so many), I've tried to name some of the people in my life who make living, even when it is very hard, feel so extraordinary to me. Thank you for the thick abundance of love and care that was/is shown to me. Your names shimmer here with my gratitude and love. Each of you has helped me discover more of who I have been and am becoming through the languages you live and transform. For the grace and courage of friendships, I'm indebted to (in alphabetical order):

Chris Abani, Hannah Aizenman, Elizabeth Alexander, Lauren K. Alleyne, Sarah Arvio, Paul Auster, Kelvyn Bell, Jen Benka, Reginald Dwayne Betts, Sherwin Bitsui, Richard Blanco, Nicholas Boggs, Cheryl Boyce Taylor, Ann Brady, Lee Briccetti, LeRonn P. Brooks, Jericho Brown, Marie Brown, Mahogany L. Browne, Erin Buckley, Margaret Busby, Christian Campbell, Cyrus Cassells, Jan Castro, Tina Chang, Francesco and Alba Clemente, Edwidge Danticat, Toi Derricotte, Kiran Desai, Natalie Diaz, K.A. Dilday, Alex Dimitrov, Gabriel Don, Rita Dove, Camille Dungy, Lisa Dwan, Cornelius Eady, Chiyuma Elliott, Cristin Ellis, Tarfia Faizullah, James Fenton, Carolyn Ferrell, Nikky Finney, Fish House Crew, David Flores, Nick Flynn, Isabel Fonseca, Santee Frazier, Dr. Joanne Gabbin, Pilar Gallego, Sarah Gambito, Suzanne Gardinier, Ross Gay, Jules Gibbs, Aracelis Girmay, Francisco Goldman, Bill Griffith, Kelle Groom, Jenny Gropp, Ellen Hagan, Nathalie Handal, Derrick Harriell, francine j. harris, Keyon Harrold, Terrance Hayes, David Haynes, Nate Heiges, Ricardo Hernandez, JP Howard, Marie Howe, Siri Hustvedt, Marcus Jackson, Mitchell Jackson, Tyehimba Jess, Amanda Johnston, Parneisha Jones, Christoph Keller, Nambi E. Kelley, Yusef Komunyakaa, Gavin Kovite, Jacqueline Jones LaMon, Eric Lane, Paul LaTorre, Rickey Laurentiis, Joseph Legaspi, David Lehman, Herbert

Leibowitz, Jan Heller Levi, Robin Coste Lewis, Ada Límon, Chip Livingston, Paul Lisicky, Anne Marie Macari, Simeon Marsalis, David Tomas Martinez, Andriniki Mattis, RaeShauna Mboma, Cecil McDonald, Rob McQuilkin, Pauline Melville, Nina Angela Mercer, Dante Micheaux, Caroline Michel, Ella Montclare, Yesenia Montilla, Kamilah Aisha Moon, Bob Morris, Paul W. Morris, Tracie Morris, Walter Mosley, David Mura, John Murillo, Ryan Murphy, Steven Murphy, Jan Murray, Walton Muyumba, Julia Myers, Angel Nafis, Marilyn Nelson, D. Nurske, Eric M. Pankey, Gregory Pardlo, Ben Pease, Laura Pegram, Willie Perdomo, Jason Peters, Carl Phillips, Tommy Pico, Darryl Pinckney, Annie Pleshette-Murphy, Iain Haley Pollock, Alice Quinn, Katie Raissian, Victoria Redel, Clarence Reynolds, Martha Rhodes, Chris Robinson, Barbara Rockman, Carey Salerno, Sonia Sanchez, Leonard Schwartz, Nicole Sealey, Vijay Seshadri, Brenda Shaughnessy, Leslie Shipman, Ira Silverberg, Taryn Simon, Oberon Sinclair, Safiya Sinclair, Tracy K. Smith, Jenny Snider, Laura Solomon, Christopher Soto, David St. John, Mary Stanley, James Thomas Stevens, Bianca Stone, Daniel Stout, Matt Taber, Craig Morgan Teicher, Paul Tran, Margaret Porter Troupe, Quincy Troupe, Carlos Uribe, Aldrin Valdez, Lyrae Van Clief-Stefanon, Sally Van Doren, Fred Viebahn, R.A. Villaneuva, Patricia Volk, Ocean Vuong, Jenisha Watts, Afaa Michael Weaver, Matthew Weiner, Simone White, Phillip B. Williams, L. Lamar Wilson, Tiphanie Yanique, and Kevin Young.

For the loss of these following beloved writers who died during the writing of this work: Meena Alexander, Maya Angelou, Linda Gregg, Monica Hand, Denis Johnson, Paule Marshall, W. S. Merwin, Toni Morrison, Mary Oliver, Paul Otremba, Marie Ponsot, Ntozake Shange, C. D. Wright, and Lucille Clifton, who died one year before my mother.

For these homes: Cave Canem Foundation, Kimbilio, Kundiman, The Millay Colony, Alice James Books, Poetry Society of America, The Furious Flower Poetry Center, The Academy of American Poets, Sarah Lawrence College, Institute of American Indian Arts, and Four Way Books.

This book was written with the generous support of Yaddo and the Robert Rauschenberg Foundation.

My thanks for the sanity, safety, and shiny toolbox we have made (and are making)—Dr. Sheldon Itzkowitz, Ph.D.

For Joy, Danny, Wendy, Jessica, and the Plumer-Robinson families. For Uncle Arthur, who I will always miss and celebrate.

For Kevin—with all my wonder, gratitude, and love. May you share your good heart with all who are lucky to know it as I have.

My sincere and incandescent gratitude to Jill Bialosky, Drew Elizabeth Weitman, and the entire team at W. W. Norton for their enthusiasm, hard work, and commitment to the publication of this book. My heartfelt gratitude to my publicist, Michelle Blankenship. Truly, it takes a village. Thank you for being mine.

I would like to especially thank my agent, Jin Auh, for her tireless support and encouragement of me. I know this book came into being, adorned in the dream of it I hoped for, because of her belief, wisdom, and hope. I would also like to thank Andrew Wylie and everyone at The Wylie Agency.

With gratitude, delight, imagination, truth, hilarity, and much else—Salman.

For my living aunts—Stephanie, Peggy Manel, Jacqueline Deneen, Ellen, Deborah, and Carolyn. For my living uncles—Arthur (Babe), Darren, Harvey, Ronald, and Mark. Also, for Uncle Michael, who died one year after my mother. He is much missed and gone far too soon. For the greats, the grands, the aunts, uncles, cousins, and kin who listen and love from the other side. For our kingdom of cousins! With special hugs for cousins Kandasi, Yazzy, Elyse, and my god-sister, Michelle (Lockard).

Finally and forever, my love and gratitude for my family—

Dad, for the sublime gift of being your daughter; my beautiful siblings, Chris, Adam, Melissa, and their loves: Leigh-Anne, Jeff, and Eumir. Ecstatically, I am an auntie, and so too, my gratitude, for my dearest baby nephew, CJ Bear—for the hope, strength, understanding, and joy all of you show me by your lives and by your love for me.

Always—Mom, I thank you with every step and breath I am given. I have tried, and am trying, to align my memory and grief into a new world without you. Please forgive whatever I didn't get right here. I can only hope, with my entire heart, that this book would mostly please you. For all that you gave to me from your fiercely beautiful heart, I love you always.